Good Grief!

This journal is designed to support you on the complex journey of grief. The purpose of this journal is to provide a safe and nurturing space where you can express your thoughts, emotions, and memories as you process your loss. By engaging with the pages you will find a compassionate companion that encourages reflection, honors the memory of your loved one, and fosters healing.

This journal belongs to:

Reminder:

They will always be apart of you.

How to process Grief

1 Acknowledge and Express Your Emotions: Feel Your Feelings Allow yourself to experience the full range of emotions, including sadness, anger, confusion, and even relief. Suppressing these emotions can delay the healing process.

---

2 Create Rituals and Memorials: Participate in or organize memorial services, celebrations of life, or other rituals that honor the memory of your loved one. Create a scrapbook, photo album, or a dedicated space in your home where you can reflect on your memories and feel connected to your loved one.

---

3 Engage in Self-Care: Maintain a routine that includes regular exercise, a healthy diet, and adequate sleep. Physical well-being can significantly impact your emotional health. Practice mindfulness, meditation, or journaling. These activities can provide a calming outlet for your thoughts and emotions.

---

4 Seek support: Consider therapy or support groups.

---

5 Find Meaning and Purpose: Engage in activities that bring you joy or a sense of accomplishment, whether it's a new hobby, volunteering, or continuing a passion you shared with your loved one. Create something in memory of your loved one, such as a charitable donation, a scholarship fund, or a piece of art. This can help you feel a sense of purpose and connection.

---

5 steps

How to cope with loneliness

YOU ARE NOT ALONE!

1	Connect with Others: Contact friends, family, or acquaintances to talk, even if it's just a quick call or text. Reaching out can remind you that you're not alone.
2	Engage in Activities You Enjoy: Spend time doing activities that bring you joy, whether it's reading, painting, gardening, or playing a musical instrument.
3	Practice Self-Compassion: Be Kind to Yourself: Acknowledge your feelings without judgment. Understand that loneliness is a common human experience and that it's okay to feel this way.
4	Self Care: Prioritize activities that nurture your body and mind, such as taking a warm bath, meditating, or journaling about your thoughts and feelings.
5	Seek Professional Help: Consider talking to a therapist or counselor who can provide support and strategies to cope with loneliness. Join support groups where you can share your experiences with others who understand what you're going through.

A Prayer For comfort

Dear Heavenly Father,

I come before You with a heart weighed down by grief and sorrow. The loss of my loved one has left an ache that words cannot describe. In this moment of profound sadness, I seek Your comforting presence. Please grant me the strength to endure the days ahead. Help me to find moments of peace and solace in the midst of my pain. Wrap me in Your loving arms and let me feel Your comforting embrace. I pray for the courage to face each new day and the grace to accept my feelings as they come. May I find healing in the cherished memories of my loved one, and let those memories bring me warmth and joy, even in the midst of my sorrow. Help me to lean on You and trust in Your unfailing love. Guide me through this valley of grief and lead me towards the light of hope and healing. I ask for Your peace to fill my heart and for Your strength to sustain me. Thank You, for being my refuge and my strength during this difficult time. I trust in Your promises and find comfort in Your presence.

In Your holy name, I pray.

Amen.

A Prayer for Healing

Dear Heavenly Father,

I come to You in my time of need, seeking Your healing touch. The pain of losing my loved one is overwhelming, and I feel lost and broken. I ask for Your grace and mercy to help mend my wounded heart. Please grant me the strength to face each day with hope. Help me to find moments of peace amidst the sorrow, and give me the courage to embrace the healing process. Surround me with Your love and let me feel Your comforting presence.

Guide me as I navigate through my grief, and help me to remember the joy and love I shared with my loved one. Let these memories be a source of comfort and strength as I heal.

I pray for patience and understanding with myself, knowing that healing is a journey. Grant me the wisdom to seek support when I need it, and the resilience to move forward one step at a time.

Fill my heart with Your peace, and help me to trust in Your plan. May Your light shine upon me, bringing hope and renewal. Thank You for being my refuge and my source of strength.

In Your holy name, I pray.

Take it one day at a time. There's no rush.

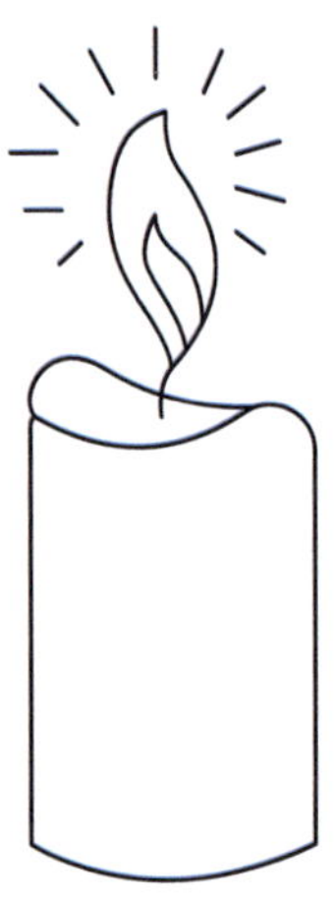

Name: ______ Date: ______

Daily Emotions Check-In

Grieving is a day-to-day process, and every day is different. For the next 30 days, you will keep track of how you are feeling. Choose two words from the list to describe how you feel today. Can't find your emotions there? Feel free to use other words.

Today, I feel: ______ ______

I think these feelings are:

- ○ both positive
- ○ positive and negative
- ○ negative and positive
- ○ both negative

I feel this way because ______

______

______

______

If I looked in a mirror right now, what expression would be on my face? Draw it in the box below:

EMOTIONS LIST

angry
annoyed
anxious
ashamed
awkward
brave
calm
cheerful
confused
discouraged
distracted
embarrassed
excited
friendly
guilty
happy
hopeful
lonely
loved
nervous
okay
sad
scared
tired
uncomfortable
unsure
worried

THE PIECES OF MY HEART

In each piece of the heart, write the name of someone you have loved and lost.

Healing from grief while deeply missing the lost can be incredibly challenging, but it is possible with time and intentional effort. Allow yourself to feel and acknowledge the pain of missing your loved one; suppressing these emotions can hinder the healing process. Embrace the memories and cherish the moments you had together, finding ways to honor their legacy through rituals, keepsakes, or traditions.

LETTERS TO HEAVEN

DATE

Dear

Sincerely,

Name:	

Date:	

Daily Emotions Check-In

Grieving is a day-to-day process, and every day is different. For the next 30 days, you will keep track of how you are feeling. Choose two words from the list to describe how you feel today. Can't find your emotions there? Feel free to use other words.

Today, I feel: ________________ ________________

I think these feelings are:

○ both positive ○ positive and negative
○ negative and positive ○ both negative

I feel this way because ______________________________
____
____
____

If I looked in a mirror right now, what expression would be on my face? Draw it in the box below:

EMOTIONS LIST

angry
annoyed
anxious
ashamed
awkward
brave
calm
cheerful
confused
discouraged
distracted
embarrassed
excited
friendly
guilty
happy
hopeful
lonely
loved
nervous
okay
sad
scared
tired
uncomfortable
unsure
worried

SELF-CARE CHECKLIST

List some things you can do in the name of self-care that will help you with the grieving and healing process. Check each item off after you complete it.

Writing Prompt

What is one lesson I learned from my loved one?
How will I continue to apply it to my life now that they're gone?

Name: ____________ Date: ____________

Daily Emotions Check-In

Grieving is a day-to-day process, and every day is different. For the next 30 days, you will keep track of how you are feeling. Choose two words from the list to describe how you feel today. Can't find your emotions there? Feel free to use other words.

Today, I feel: ____________ ____________

I think these feelings are:

- ○ both positive
- ○ positive and negative
- ○ negative and positive
- ○ both negative

I feel this way because ____________

____

____

____

If I looked in a mirror right now, what expression would be on my face? Draw it in the box below:

EMOTIONS LIST

angry
annoyed
anxious
ashamed
awkward
brave
calm
cheerful
confused
discouraged
distracted
embarrassed
excited
friendly
guilty
happy
hopeful
lonely
loved
nervous
okay
sad
scared
tired
uncomfortable
unsure
worried

My Support Circle

List people you can call on when you're in need. Grieving is hard and you shouldn't have to do it alone. You are going to need your circle.

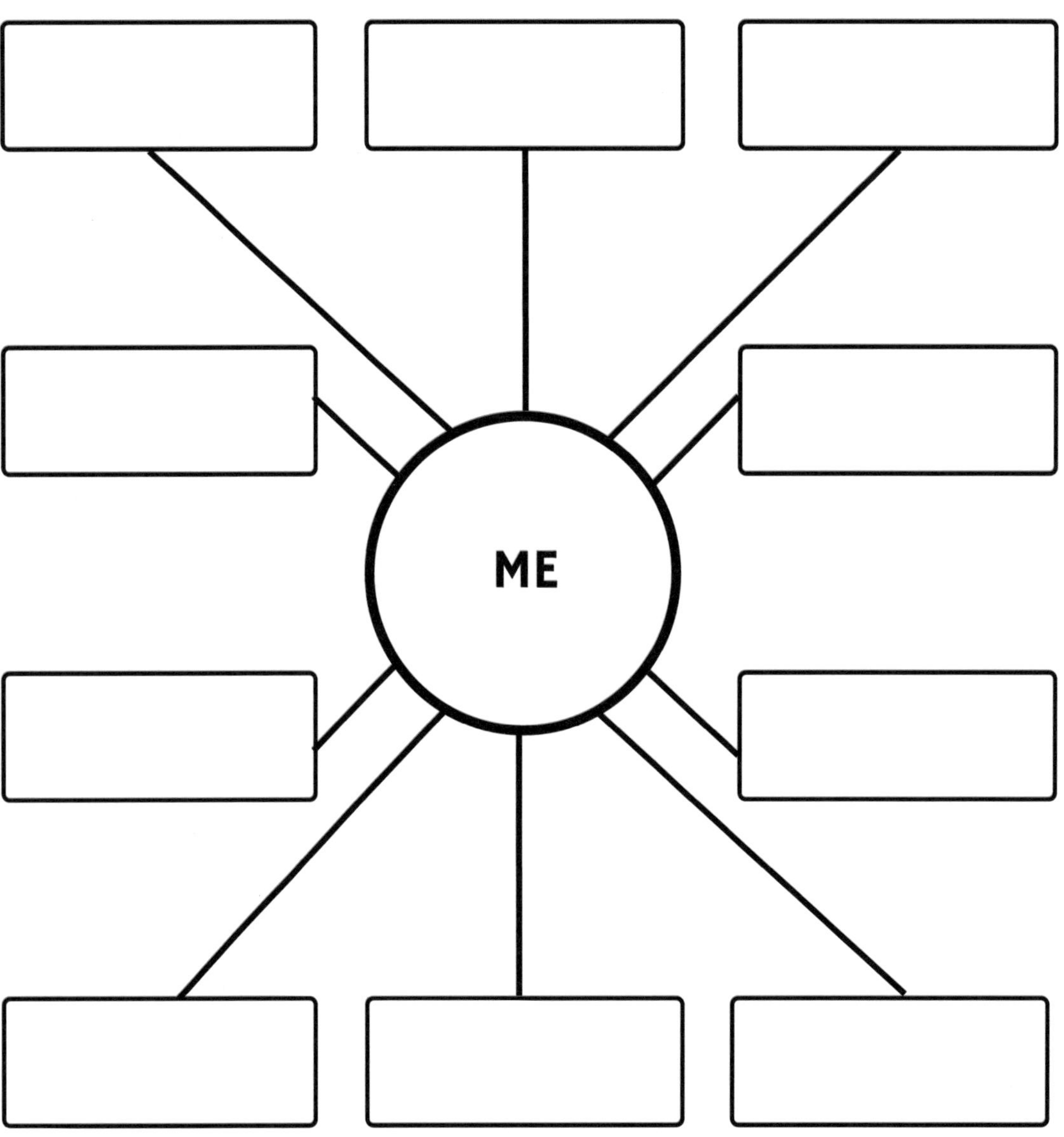

Healing Day by Day

Today, I felt:

Today, I thought about you and:

Today, I needed:

Today, I decided to:

Today, I discovered this about myself:

Name: ____________ Date: ____________

Daily Emotions Check-In

Grieving is a day-to-day process, and every day is different. For the next 30 days, you will keep track of how you are feeling. Choose two words from the list to describe how you feel today. Can't find your emotions there? Feel free to use other words.

Today, I feel: ____________ ____________

I think these feelings are:

- ○ both positive
- ○ positive and negative
- ○ negative and positive
- ○ both negative

I feel this way because ____________

____

____

____

If I looked in a mirror right now, what expression would be on my face? Draw it in the box below:

EMOTIONS LIST

angry
annoyed
anxious
ashamed
awkward
brave
calm
cheerful
confused
discouraged
distracted
embarrassed
excited
friendly
guilty
happy
hopeful
lonely
loved
nervous
okay
sad
scared
tired
uncomfortable
unsure
worried

THE COLORS OF GRIEF

REMINDER: HEALING TAKES TIME.

After you've completed coloring the image, answer the following questions:

What thoughts and feelings arose as you colored the image?

Did you find it calming or challenging to stay focused on coloring?

How do you feel now?

If I wrote a book about You...

Your lost loved one is the character in this story. Write about them.
Write about who they were to you and what you'll miss the most.
Remembering them in a positive light will help you on the healing journey.

When we meet again, I will feel:

____

____

____

____

____

Healing begins when we allow our hearts to feel and our souls to remember.

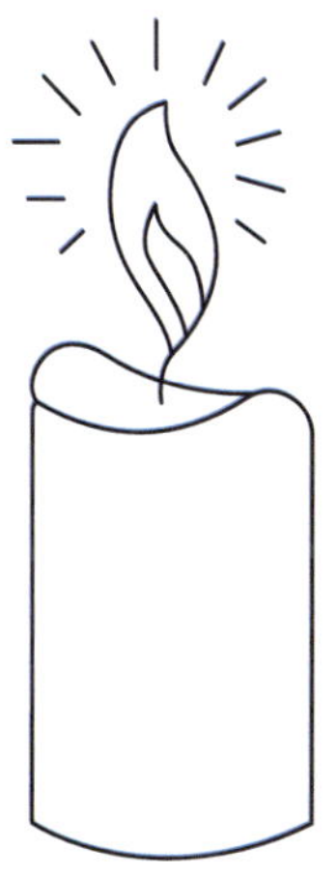

Name: ______________ Date: ______________

Daily Emotions Check-In

Grieving is a day-to-day process, and every day is different. For the next 30 days, you will keep track of how you are feeling. Choose two words from the list to describe how you feel today. Can't find your emotions there? Feel free to use other words.

Today, I feel: ______________ ______________

I think these feelings are:

- ○ both positive
- ○ positive and negative
- ○ negative and positive
- ○ both negative

I feel this way because ______________

____

____

____

If I looked in a mirror right now, what expression would be on my face? Draw it in the box below:

EMOTIONS LIST

angry
annoyed
anxious
ashamed
awkward
brave
calm
cheerful
confused
discouraged
distracted
embarrassed
excited
friendly
guilty
happy
hopeful
lonely
loved
nervous
okay
sad
scared
tired
uncomfortable
unsure
worried

Writing Prompt

How can I honor the memories of my loved ones in my daily life?

Healing Day by Day

Today, I felt:

Today, I thought about you and:

Today, I needed:

Today, I decided to:

Today, I discovered this about myself:

Name: ____________ Date: ____________

Daily Emotions Check-In

Grieving is a day-to-day process, and every day is different. For the next 30 days, you will keep track of how you are feeling. Choose two words from the list to describe how you feel today. Can't find your emotions there? Feel free to use other words.

Today, I feel: ____________ ____________

I think these feelings are:

- ○ both positive
- ○ positive and negative
- ○ negative and positive
- ○ both negative

I feel this way because ____________

____

____

____

If I looked in a mirror right now, what expression would be on my face? Draw it in the box below:

EMOTIONS LIST

angry
annoyed
anxious
ashamed
awkward
brave
calm
cheerful
confused
discouraged
distracted
embarrassed
excited
friendly
guilty
happy
hopeful
lonely
loved
nervous
okay
sad
scared
tired
uncomfortable
unsure
worried

LETTERS TO HEAVEN

DATE

Dear

Sincerely,

Name: ____________ Date: ____________

Daily Emotions Check-In

Grieving is a day-to-day process, and every day is different. For the next 30 days, you will keep track of how you are feeling. Choose two words from the list to describe how you feel today. Can't find your emotions there? Feel free to use other words.

Today, I feel: ____________ ____________

I think these feelings are:

- ○ both positive
- ○ positive and negative
- ○ negative and positive
- ○ both negative

I feel this way because ____________________

____

____

____

If I looked in a mirror right now, what expression would be on my face? Draw it in the box below:

EMOTIONS LIST

angry
annoyed
anxious
ashamed
awkward
brave
calm
cheerful
confused
discouraged
distracted
embarrassed
excited
friendly
guilty
happy
hopeful
lonely
loved
nervous
okay
sad
scared
tired
uncomfortable
unsure
worried

THE COLORS OF GRIEF

REMINDER: HEALING TAKES TIME.

After you've completed coloring the image, answer the following questions:

What thoughts and feelings arose as you colored the image?

Did you find it calming or challenging to stay focused on coloring?

How do you feel now?

Name: ______ Date: ______

Daily Emotions Check-In

Grieving is a day-to-day process, and every day is different. For the next 30 days, you will keep track of how you are feeling. Choose two words from the list to describe how you feel today. Can't find your emotions there? Feel free to use other words.

Today, I feel: ______ ______

I think these feelings are:

- ○ both positive
- ○ positive and negative
- ○ negative and positive
- ○ both negative

I feel this way because ______

______

______

______

If I looked in a mirror right now, what expression would be on my face? Draw it in the box below:

EMOTIONS LIST

angry
annoyed
anxious
ashamed
awkward
brave
calm
cheerful
confused
discouraged
distracted
embarrassed
excited
friendly
guilty
happy
hopeful
lonely
loved
nervous
okay
sad
scared
tired
uncomfortable
unsure
worried

Writing Prompt

What are the hardest parts of your daily life since losing your loved one? How have you been coping with these changes?

Moving forward doesn't mean forgetting.

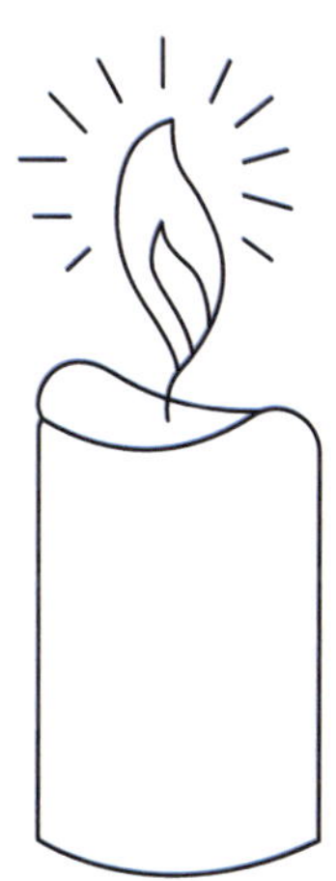

Name: ____________ Date: ____________

Daily Emotions Check-In

Grieving is a day-to-day process, and every day is different. For the next 30 days, you will keep track of how you are feeling. Choose two words from the list to describe how you feel today. Can't find your emotions there? Feel free to use other words.

Today, I feel: ______________ ______________

I think these feelings are:

- ○ both positive
- ○ positive and negative
- ○ negative and positive
- ○ both negative

I feel this way because ______________________________

____

____

____

If I looked in a mirror right now, what expression would be on my face? Draw it in the box below:

EMOTIONS LIST

angry
annoyed
anxious
ashamed
awkward
brave
calm
cheerful
confused
discouraged
distracted
embarrassed
excited
friendly
guilty
happy
hopeful
lonely
loved
nervous
okay
sad
scared
tired
uncomfortable
unsure
worried

MEMORY BOX

Fill the boxes with memories you have of your loved one. Be sure to include memories that make you smile or laugh.

Name of loved one: ______________________________

Name: ____________ Date: ____________

Daily Emotions Check-In

Grieving is a day-to-day process, and every day is different. For the next 30 days, you will keep track of how you are feeling. Choose two words from the list to describe how you feel today. Can't find your emotions there? Feel free to use other words.

Today, I feel: ____________ ____________

I think these feelings are:

- ○ both positive
- ○ positive and negative
- ○ negative and positive
- ○ both negative

I feel this way because ____________

____

____

____

If I looked in a mirror right now, what expression would be on my face? Draw it in the box below:

EMOTIONS LIST

angry
annoyed
anxious
ashamed
awkward
brave
calm
cheerful
confused
discouraged
distracted
embarrassed
excited
friendly
guilty
happy
hopeful
lonely
loved
nervous
okay
sad
scared
tired
uncomfortable
unsure
worried

DOWN MEMORY LANE

Complete this maze as you take a trip down memory lane.
Think about your loved one and the very first memory you have of them.

May your memories give you comfort
in your time of need.

LETTERS TO HEAVEN

DATE

Dear

Sincerely,

Name: ____________ Date: ____________

Daily Emotions Check-In

Grieving is a day-to-day process, and every day is different. For the next 30 days, you will keep track of how you are feeling. Choose two words from the list to describe how you feel today. Can't find your emotions there? Feel free to use other words.

Today, I feel: ____________ ____________

I think these feelings are:

- ○ both positive
- ○ positive and negative
- ○ negative and positive
- ○ both negative

I feel this way because ____________________

____

____

____

If I looked in a mirror right now, what expression would be on my face? Draw it in the box below:

EMOTIONS LIST

angry
annoyed
anxious
ashamed
awkward
brave
calm
cheerful
confused
discouraged
distracted
embarrassed
excited
friendly
guilty
happy
hopeful
lonely
loved
nervous
okay
sad
scared
tired
uncomfortable
unsure
worried

Healing Day by Day

Today, I felt:

Today, I thought about you and:

Today, I needed:

Today, I decided to:

Today, I discovered this about myself:

Name: ______________ Date: ______________

Daily Emotions Check-In

Grieving is a day-to-day process, and every day is different. For the next 30 days, you will keep track of how you are feeling. Choose two words from the list to describe how you feel today. Can't find your emotions there? Feel free to use other words.

Today, I feel: ______________ ______________

I think these feelings are:

- ○ both positive
- ○ positive and negative
- ○ negative and positive
- ○ both negative

I feel this way because ______________________________

____

____

____

If I looked in a mirror right now, what expression would be on my face? Draw it in the box below:

EMOTIONS LIST

angry
annoyed
anxious
ashamed
awkward
brave
calm
cheerful
confused
discouraged
distracted
embarrassed
excited
friendly
guilty
happy
hopeful
lonely
loved
nervous
okay
sad
scared
tired
uncomfortable
unsure
worried

THE COLORS OF GRIEF

REMINDER: HEALING TAKES TIME.

After you've completed coloring the image, answer the following questions:

What thoughts and feelings arose as you colored the image?

Did you find it calming or challenging to stay focused on coloring?

How do you feel now?

Name: ____________ Date: ____________

Daily Emotions Check-In

Grieving is a day-to-day process, and every day is different. For the next 30 days, you will keep track of how you are feeling. Choose two words from the list to describe how you feel today. Can't find your emotions there? Feel free to use other words.

Today, I feel: ____________ ____________

I think these feelings are:

- ○ both positive
- ○ positive and negative
- ○ negative and positive
- ○ both negative

I feel this way because ____________________

____

____

____

If I looked in a mirror right now, what expression would be on my face? Draw it in the box below:

EMOTIONS LIST

angry
annoyed
anxious
ashamed
awkward
brave
calm
cheerful
confused
discouraged
distracted
embarrassed
excited
friendly
guilty
happy
hopeful
lonely
loved
nervous
okay
sad
scared
tired
uncomfortable
unsure
worried

Writing Prompt

Describe a moment when you felt the presence of a loved one after they were gone. How did it affect you?

Grief is a chapter, not the whole story; healing writes the next page.

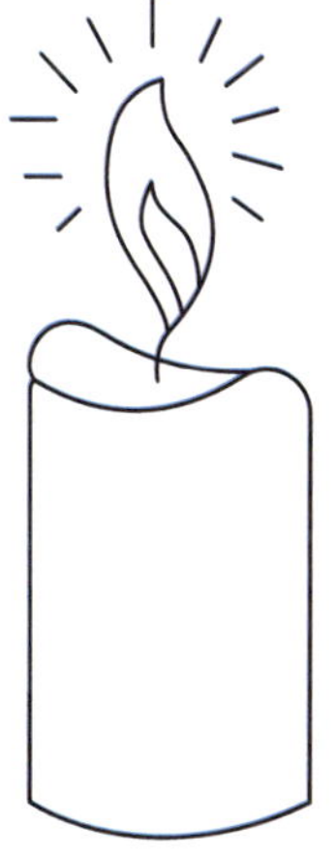

Name:

Date:

Daily Emotions Check-In

Grieving is a day-to-day process, and every day is different. For the next 30 days, you will keep track of how you are feeling. Choose two words from the list to describe how you feel today. Can't find your emotions there? Feel free to use other words.

Today, I feel: ________________ ________________

I think these feelings are:

○ both positive ○ positive and negative
○ negative and positive ○ both negative

I feel this way because ______________________________
____
____
____

If I looked in a mirror right now, what expression would be on my face? Draw it in the box below:

EMOTIONS LIST

angry
annoyed
anxious
ashamed
awkward
brave
calm
cheerful
confused
discouraged
distracted
embarrassed
excited
friendly
guilty
happy
hopeful
lonely
loved
nervous
okay
sad
scared
tired
uncomfortable
unsure
worried

LETTERS TO HEAVEN

DATE

Dear

Sincerely,

Name: ____________ Date: ____________

Daily Emotions Check-In

Grieving is a day-to-day process, and every day is different. For the next 30 days, you will keep track of how you are feeling. Choose two words from the list to describe how you feel today. Can't find your emotions there? Feel free to use other words.

Today, I feel: ____________ ____________

I think these feelings are:

- ○ both positive
- ○ positive and negative
- ○ negative and positive
- ○ both negative

I feel this way because ____________________

____

____

____

If I looked in a mirror right now, what expression would be on my face? Draw it in the box below:

EMOTIONS LIST

angry
annoyed
anxious
ashamed
awkward
brave
calm
cheerful
confused
discouraged
distracted
embarrassed
excited
friendly
guilty
happy
hopeful
lonely
loved
nervous
okay
sad
scared
tired
uncomfortable
unsure
worried

Healing Day by Day

Today, I felt:

Today, I thought about you and:

Today, I needed:

Today, I decided to:

Today, I discovered this about myself:

Name: ____________________ Date: ____________________

Daily Emotions Check-In

Grieving is a day-to-day process, and every day is different. For the next 30 days, you will keep track of how you are feeling. Choose two words from the list to describe how you feel today. Can't find your emotions there? Feel free to use other words.

Today, I feel: ______________ ______________

I think these feelings are:

○ both positive ○ positive and negative
○ negative and positive ○ both negative

I feel this way because ____________________

____

____

____

If I looked in a mirror right now, what expression would be on my face? Draw it in the box below:

EMOTIONS LIST

angry
annoyed
anxious
ashamed
awkward
brave
calm
cheerful
confused
discouraged
distracted
embarrassed
excited
friendly
guilty
happy
hopeful
lonely
loved
nervous
okay
sad
scared
tired
uncomfortable
unsure
worried

Writing Prompt

Write about a time when you felt a sense of peace or comfort during your grieving process. What brought about that feeling?

Name: ____________

Date: ____________

Daily Emotions Check-In

Grieving is a day-to-day process, and every day is different. For the next 30 days, you will keep track of how you are feeling. Choose two words from the list to describe how you feel today. Can't find your emotions there? Feel free to use other words.

Today, I feel: ____________ ____________

I think these feelings are:

- ○ both positive
- ○ positive and negative
- ○ negative and positive
- ○ both negative

I feel this way because ____________

____

____

____

If I looked in a mirror right now, what expression would be on my face? Draw it in the box below:

EMOTIONS LIST

angry
annoyed
anxious
ashamed
awkward
brave
calm
cheerful
confused
discouraged
distracted
embarrassed
excited
friendly
guilty
happy
hopeful
lonely
loved
nervous
okay
sad
scared
tired
uncomfortable
unsure
worried

THE COLORS OF GRIEF

REMINDER: HEALING TAKES TIME.

After you've completed coloring the image, answer the following questions:

What thoughts and feelings arose as you colored the image?

Did you find it calming or challenging to stay focused on coloring?

How do you feel now?

Name: ____________

Date: ____________

Daily Emotions Check-In

Grieving is a day-to-day process, and every day is different. For the next 30 days, you will keep track of how you are feeling. Choose two words from the list to describe how you feel today. Can't find your emotions there? Feel free to use other words.

Today, I feel: ____________ ____________

I think these feelings are:

- ○ both positive
- ○ positive and negative
- ○ negative and positive
- ○ both negative

I feel this way because ____________

____

____

____

If I looked in a mirror right now, what expression would be on my face? Draw it in the box below:

EMOTIONS LIST

angry
annoyed
anxious
ashamed
awkward
brave
calm
cheerful
confused
discouraged
distracted
embarrassed
excited
friendly
guilty
happy
hopeful
lonely
loved
nervous
okay
sad
scared
tired
uncomfortable
unsure
worried

Healing Day by Day

Today, I felt:

Today, I thought about you and:

Today, I needed:

Today, I decided to:

Today, I discovered this about myself:

Name: ____________ Date: ____________

Daily Emotions Check-In

Grieving is a day-to-day process, and every day is different. For the next 30 days, you will keep track of how you are feeling. Choose two words from the list to describe how you feel today. Can't find your emotions there? Feel free to use other words.

Today, I feel: ____________ ____________

I think these feelings are:

- ○ both positive
- ○ positive and negative
- ○ negative and positive
- ○ both negative

I feel this way because ____________

____

____

____

If I looked in a mirror right now, what expression would be on my face? Draw it in the box below:

EMOTIONS LIST

angry
annoyed
anxious
ashamed
awkward
brave
calm
cheerful
confused
discouraged
distracted
embarrassed
excited
friendly
guilty
happy
hopeful
lonely
loved
nervous
okay
sad
scared
tired
uncomfortable
unsure
worried

Writing Prompt

List five ways you can honor your loved one's memory and incorporate their legacy into your life.

Name: ____________ Date: ____________

Daily Emotions Check-In

Grieving is a day-to-day process, and every day is different. For the next 30 days, you will keep track of how you are feeling. Choose two words from the list to describe how you feel today. Can't find your emotions there? Feel free to use other words.

Today, I feel: ____________ ____________

I think these feelings are:

- ○ both positive
- ○ positive and negative
- ○ negative and positive
- ○ both negative

I feel this way because ____________

____

____

____

If I looked in a mirror right now, what expression would be on my face? Draw it in the box below:

EMOTIONS LIST

angry
annoyed
anxious
ashamed
awkward
brave
calm
cheerful
confused
discouraged
distracted
embarrassed
excited
friendly
guilty
happy
hopeful
lonely
loved
nervous
okay
sad
scared
tired
uncomfortable
unsure
worried

Healing Day by Day

Today, I felt:

Today, I thought about you and:

Today, I needed:

Today, I decided to:

Today, I discovered this about myself:

It's okay to cry. Cry as much as you need to.

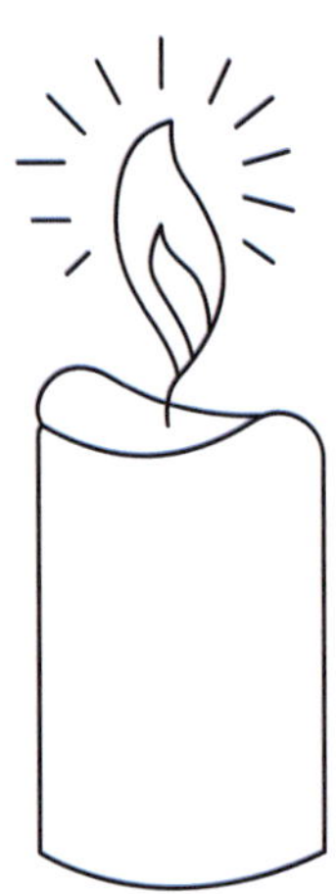

Name:	

Date:	

Daily Emotions Check-In

Grieving is a day-to-day process, and every day is different. For the next 30 days, you will keep track of how you are feeling. Choose two words from the list to describe how you feel today. Can't find your emotions there? Feel free to use other words.

Today, I feel: ______________ ______________

I think these feelings are:

- ○ both positive
- ○ positive and negative
- ○ negative and positive
- ○ both negative

I feel this way because ______________________

____

____

____

If I looked in a mirror right now, what expression would be on my face? Draw it in the box below:

EMOTIONS LIST

angry
annoyed
anxious
ashamed
awkward
brave
calm
cheerful
confused
discouraged
distracted
embarrassed
excited
friendly
guilty
happy
hopeful
lonely
loved
nervous
okay
sad
scared
tired
uncomfortable
unsure
worried

LETTERS TO HEAVEN

DATE

Dear

Sincerely,

Name: ____________ Date: ____________

Daily Emotions Check-In

Grieving is a day-to-day process, and every day is different. For the next 30 days, you will keep track of how you are feeling. Choose two words from the list to describe how you feel today. Can't find your emotions there? Feel free to use other words.

Today, I feel: ____________ ____________

I think these feelings are:

- ○ both positive
- ○ positive and negative
- ○ negative and positive
- ○ both negative

I feel this way because ______________________________

____

____

____

If I looked in a mirror right now, what expression would be on my face? Draw it in the box below:

EMOTIONS LIST

angry
annoyed
anxious
ashamed
awkward
brave
calm
cheerful
confused
discouraged
distracted
embarrassed
excited
friendly
guilty
happy
hopeful
lonely
loved
nervous
okay
sad
scared
tired
uncomfortable
unsure
worried

Writing Prompt

Write a letter of forgiveness, either to yourself or someone else, related to your grief. What do you need to let go of to heal?

Name: ____________ Date: ____________

Daily Emotions Check-In

Grieving is a day-to-day process, and every day is different. For the next 30 days, you will keep track of how you are feeling. Choose two words from the list to describe how you feel today. Can't find your emotions there? Feel free to use other words.

Today, I feel: ______________ ______________

I think these feelings are:

- ○ both positive
- ○ positive and negative
- ○ negative and positive
- ○ both negative

I feel this way because ______________________________

____

____

____

If I looked in a mirror right now, what expression would be on my face? Draw it in the box below:

EMOTIONS LIST

angry
annoyed
anxious
ashamed
awkward
brave
calm
cheerful
confused
discouraged
distracted
embarrassed
excited
friendly
guilty
happy
hopeful
lonely
loved
nervous
okay
sad
scared
tired
uncomfortable
unsure
worried

Writing Prompt

Reflect on the ways you've grown or changed since your loss.
How has this experience shaped you?

Name:

Date:

Daily Emotions Check-In

Grieving is a day-to-day process, and every day is different. For the next 30 days, you will keep track of how you are feeling. Choose two words from the list to describe how you feel today. Can't find your emotions there? Feel free to use other words.

Today, I feel: ____________ ____________

I think these feelings are:

- ○ both positive
- ○ positive and negative
- ○ negative and positive
- ○ both negative

I feel this way because ____________

If I looked in a mirror right now, what expression would be on my face? Draw it in the box below:

EMOTIONS LIST

angry
annoyed
anxious
ashamed
awkward
brave
calm
cheerful
confused
discouraged
distracted
embarrassed
excited
friendly
guilty
happy
hopeful
lonely
loved
nervous
okay
sad
scared
tired
uncomfortable
unsure
worried

THE COLORS OF GRIEF

REMINDER: HEALING TAKES TIME.

After you've completed coloring the image, answer the following questions:

What thoughts and feelings arose as you colored the image?

Did you find it calming or challenging to stay focused on coloring?

How do you feel now?

Name:	

Date:	

Daily Emotions Check-In

Grieving is a day-to-day process, and every day is different. For the next 30 days, you will keep track of how you are feeling. Choose two words from the list to describe how you feel today. Can't find your emotions there? Feel free to use other words.

Today, I feel: ________________ ________________

I think these feelings are:

- ○ both positive
- ○ positive and negative
- ○ negative and positive
- ○ both negative

I feel this way because ______________________________

____

____

____

If I looked in a mirror right now, what expression would be on my face? Draw it in the box below:

EMOTIONS LIST

angry
annoyed
anxious
ashamed
awkward
brave
calm
cheerful
confused
discouraged
distracted
embarrassed
excited
friendly
guilty
happy
hopeful
lonely
loved
nervous
okay
sad
scared
tired
uncomfortable
unsure
worried

Healing Day by Day

Today, I felt:

Today, I thought about you and:

Today, I needed:

Today, I decided to:

Today, I discovered this about myself:

Name: ____________ Date: ____________

Daily Emotions Check-In

Grieving is a day-to-day process, and every day is different. For the next 30 days, you will keep track of how you are feeling. Choose two words from the list to describe how you feel today. Can't find your emotions there? Feel free to use other words.

Today, I feel: ____________ ____________

I think these feelings are:

○ both positive ○ positive and negative
○ negative and positive ○ both negative

I feel this way because ____________________

____

____

____

If I looked in a mirror right now, what expression would be on my face? Draw it in the box below:

EMOTIONS LIST

angry
annoyed
anxious
ashamed
awkward
brave
calm
cheerful
confused
discouraged
distracted
embarrassed
excited
friendly
guilty
happy
hopeful
lonely
loved
nervous
okay
sad
scared
tired
uncomfortable
unsure
worried

Writing Prompt

Imagine a future where you have found peace with your loss.
What does that future look like? How do you feel?

“The good news is that one day you will meet again.”

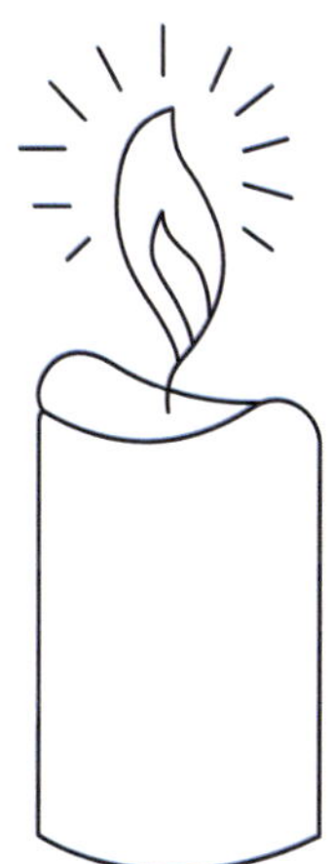

Name: ____________ Date: ____________

Daily Emotions Check-In

Grieving is a day-to-day process, and every day is different. For the next 30 days, you will keep track of how you are feeling. Choose two words from the list to describe how you feel today. Can't find your emotions there? Feel free to use other words.

Today, I feel: ____________ ____________

I think these feelings are:

- ○ both positive
- ○ positive and negative
- ○ negative and positive
- ○ both negative

I feel this way because ____________

____

____

____

If I looked in a mirror right now, what expression would be on my face? Draw it in the box below:

EMOTIONS LIST

angry
annoyed
anxious
ashamed
awkward
brave
calm
cheerful
confused
discouraged
distracted
embarrassed
excited
friendly
guilty
happy
hopeful
lonely
loved
nervous
okay
sad
scared
tired
uncomfortable
unsure
worried

THE COLORS OF GRIEF

REMINDER: HEALING TAKES TIME.

After you've completed coloring the image, answer the following questions:

What thoughts and feelings arose as you colored the image?

Did you find it calming or challenging to stay focused on coloring?

How do you feel now?

LETTERS TO HEAVEN

DATE

Dear

Sincerely,

Name: ______________________ Date: ______________________

Daily Emotions Check-In

Grieving is a day-to-day process, and every day is different. For the next 30 days, you will keep track of how you are feeling. Choose two words from the list to describe how you feel today. Can't find your emotions there? Feel free to use other words.

Today, I feel: ______________ ______________

I think these feelings are:

- ○ both positive
- ○ positive and negative
- ○ negative and positive
- ○ both negative

I feel this way because ______________________

____

____

____

If I looked in a mirror right now, what expression would be on my face? Draw it in the box below:

EMOTIONS LIST

angry
annoyed
anxious
ashamed
awkward
brave
calm
cheerful
confused
discouraged
distracted
embarrassed
excited
friendly
guilty
happy
hopeful
lonely
loved
nervous
okay
sad
scared
tired
uncomfortable
unsure
worried

Writing Prompt

Describe a new hobby or activity you've taken up since your loss.
How does it help you in your healing process?

Name: ____________ Date: ____________

Daily Emotions Check-In

Grieving is a day-to-day process, and every day is different. For the next 30 days, you will keep track of how you are feeling. Choose two words from the list to describe how you feel today. Can't find your emotions there? Feel free to use other words.

Today, I feel: ______________ ______________

I think these feelings are:

○ both positive ○ positive and negative
○ negative and positive ○ both negative

I feel this way because ______________________

____

____

____

If I looked in a mirror right now, what expression would be on my face? Draw it in the box below:

EMOTIONS LIST

angry
annoyed
anxious
ashamed
awkward
brave
calm
cheerful
confused
discouraged
distracted
embarrassed
excited
friendly
guilty
happy
hopeful
lonely
loved
nervous
okay
sad
scared
tired
uncomfortable
unsure
worried

Gratitude Jar

Write everything you are thankful for today inside the jar.

THE COLORS OF GRIEF

REMINDER: HEALING TAKES TIME.

After you've completed coloring the image, answer the following questions:

What thoughts and feelings arose as you colored the image?

Did you find it calming or challenging to stay focused on coloring?

How do you feel now?

Name: ____________ Date: ____________

Daily Emotions Check-In

Grieving is a day-to-day process, and every day is different. For the next 30 days, you will keep track of how you are feeling. Choose two words from the list to describe how you feel today. Can't find your emotions there? Feel free to use other words.

Today, I feel: ____________ ____________

I think these feelings are:

- ○ both positive
- ○ positive and negative
- ○ negative and positive
- ○ both negative

I feel this way because ____________

____

____

____

If I looked in a mirror right now, what expression would be on my face? Draw it in the box below:

EMOTIONS LIST

angry
annoyed
anxious
ashamed
awkward
brave
calm
cheerful
confused
discouraged
distracted
embarrassed
excited
friendly
guilty
happy
hopeful
lonely
loved
nervous
okay
sad
scared
tired
uncomfortable
unsure
worried

LETTERS TO HEAVEN

DATE

Dear

Sincerely,

Daily Journaling

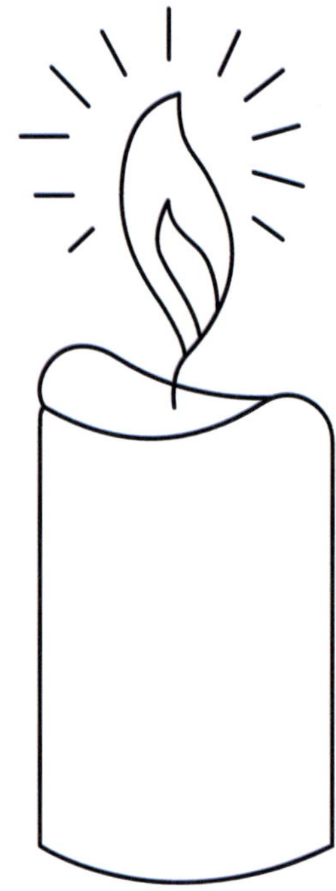

Daily Journal

Date:

Daily Journal

Date:

Daily Journal

Date:

Daily Journal

Date:

Daily Journal

Date:

Daily Journal

Date:

Daily Journal

Date:

Daily Journal

Date:

Daily Journal

Date:

Daily Journal

Date:

Daily Journal

Date:

Daily Journal

Date:

Daily Journal

Date:

Daily Journal

Date:

Daily Journal

Date:

Daily Journal

Date:

Daily Journal

Date:

Daily Journal

Date:

Daily Journal

Date:

Daily Journal

Date:

Daily Journal

Date:

Daily Journal

Date:

Daily Journal

Date:

Daily Journal

Date:

Daily Journal

Date:

Daily Journal

Date:

Daily Journal

Date:

Daily Journal

Date:

Daily Journal

Date:

Daily Journal

Date:

Daily Journal

Date: